AFRAID

by Robin Nelson

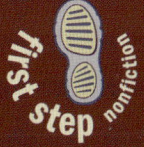

Lerner Publications Company · Minneapolis

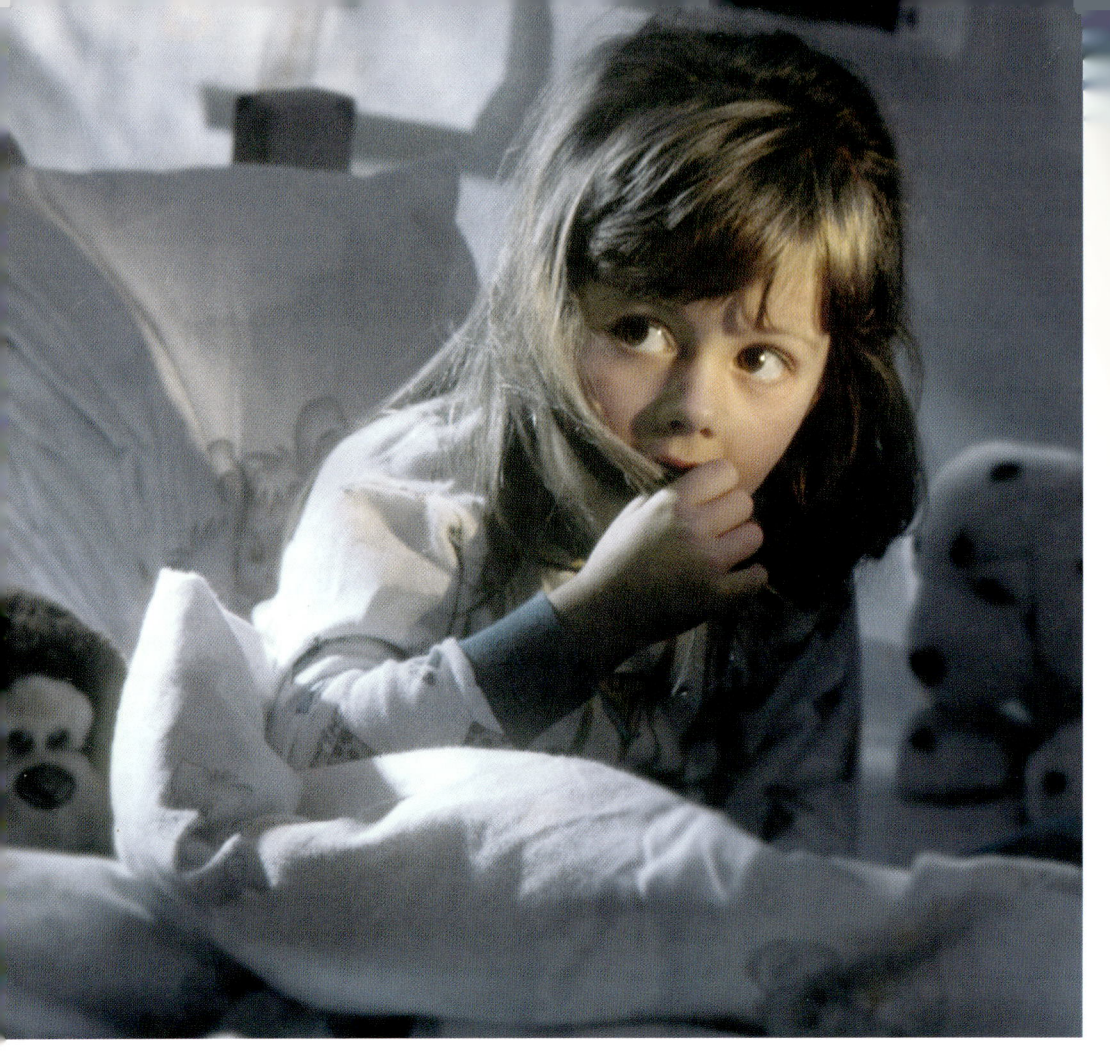

What makes me afraid?

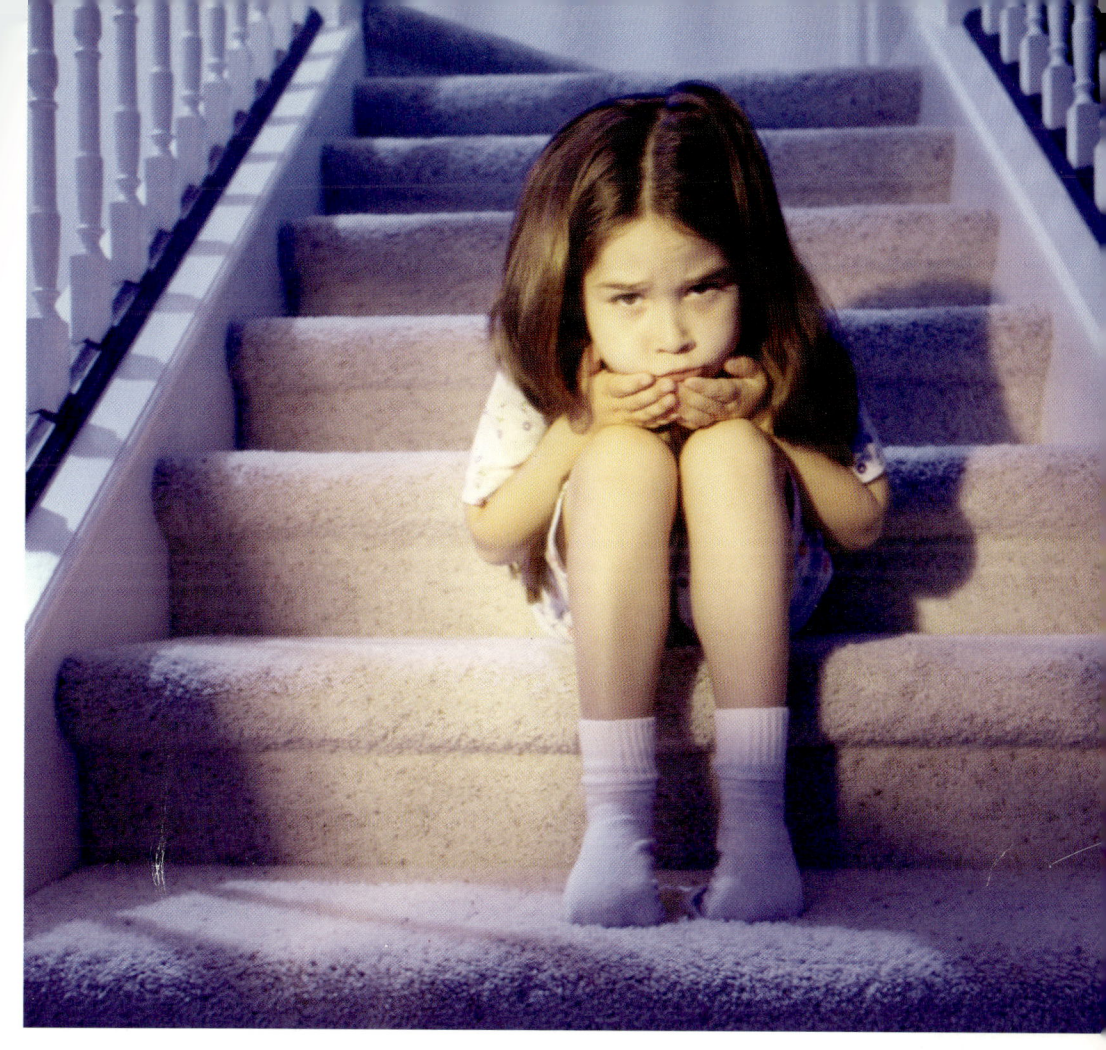

The dark

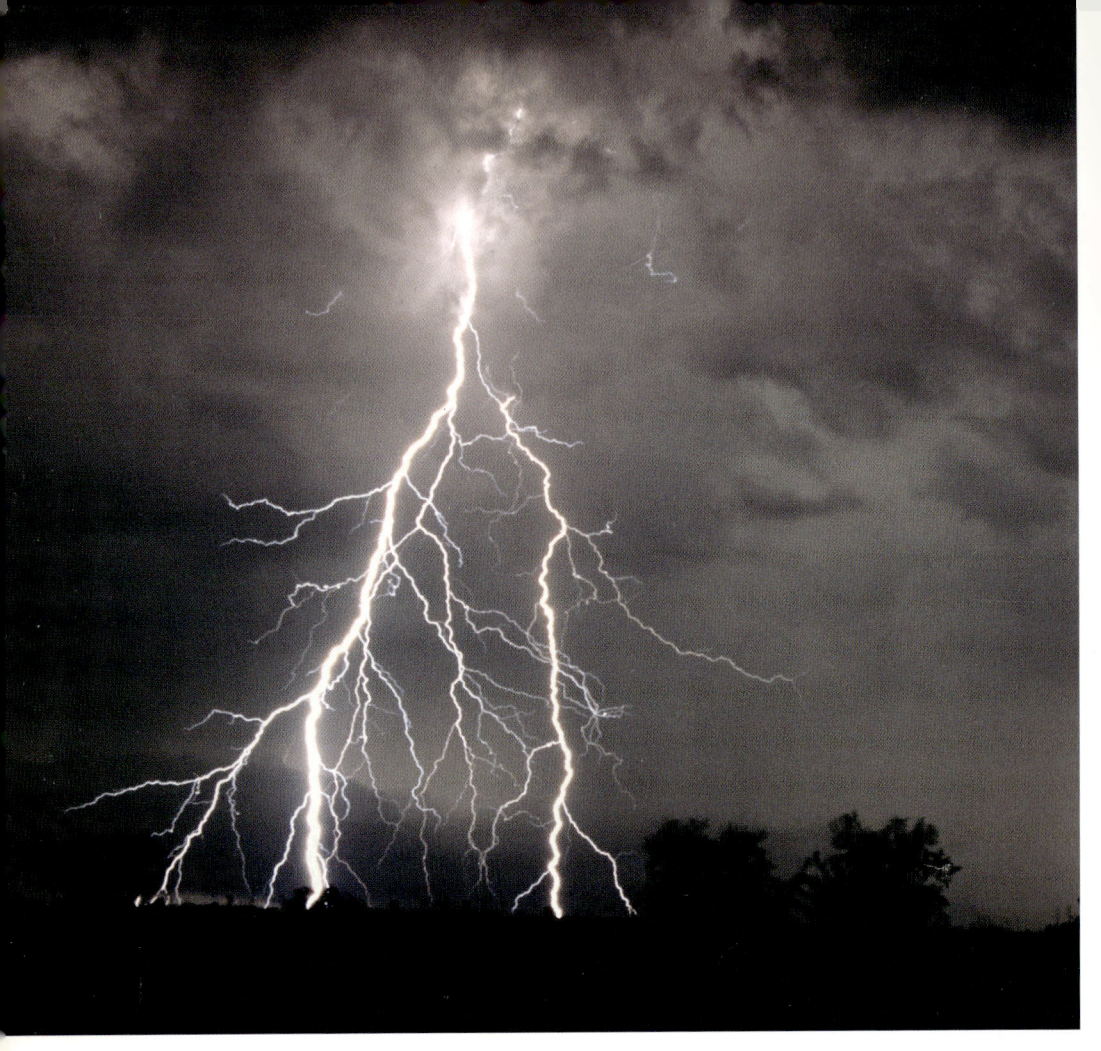

Storms

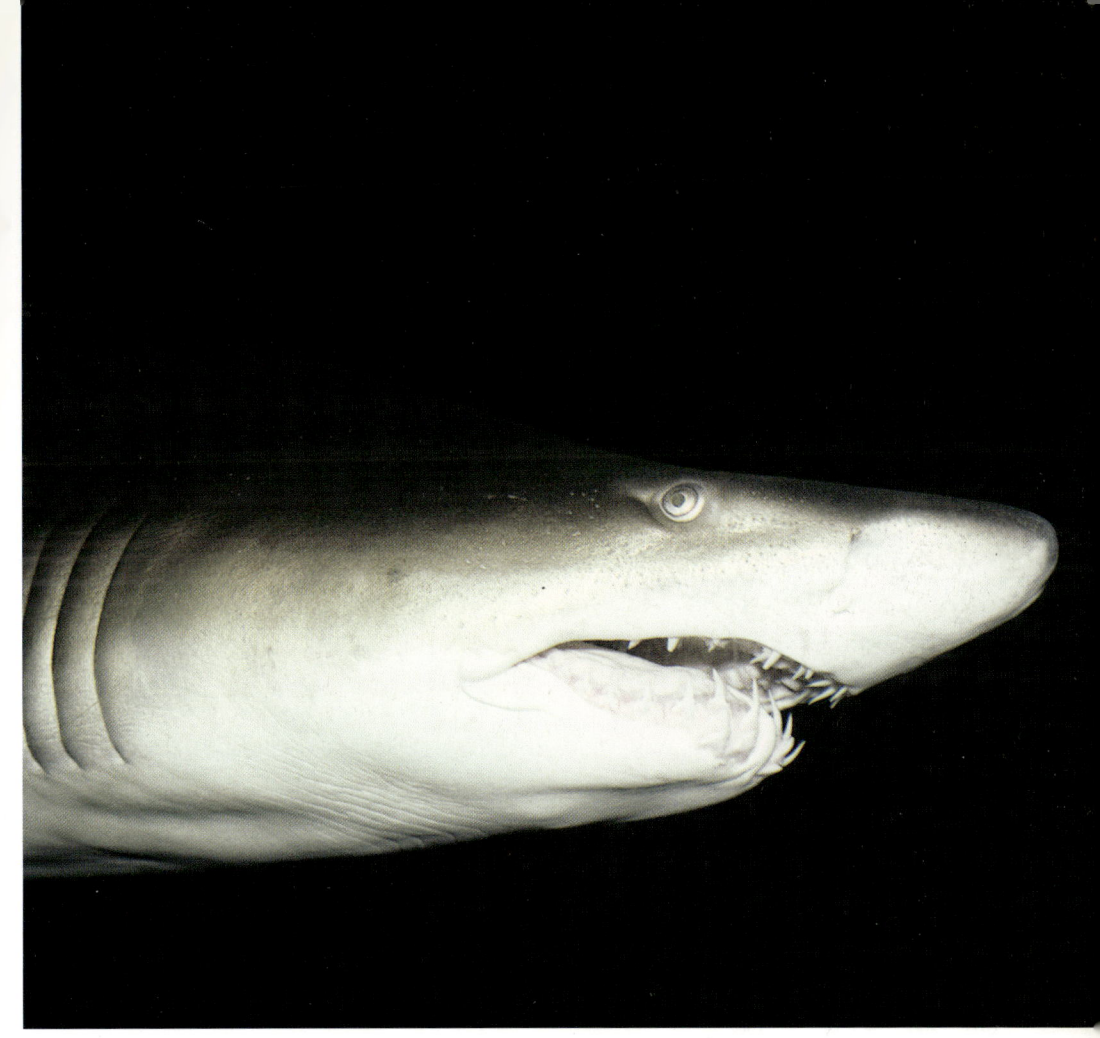

Sharks

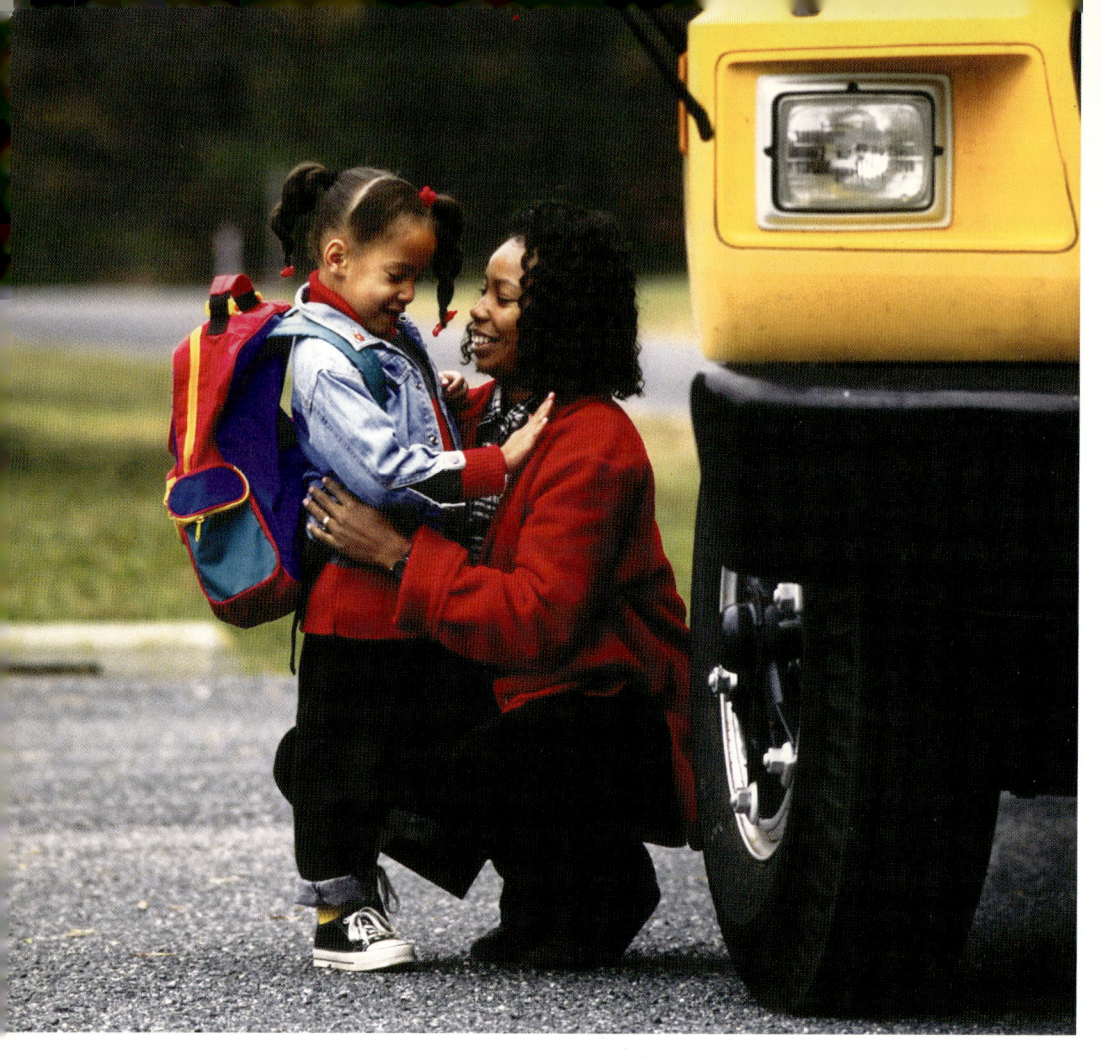

The first day of school

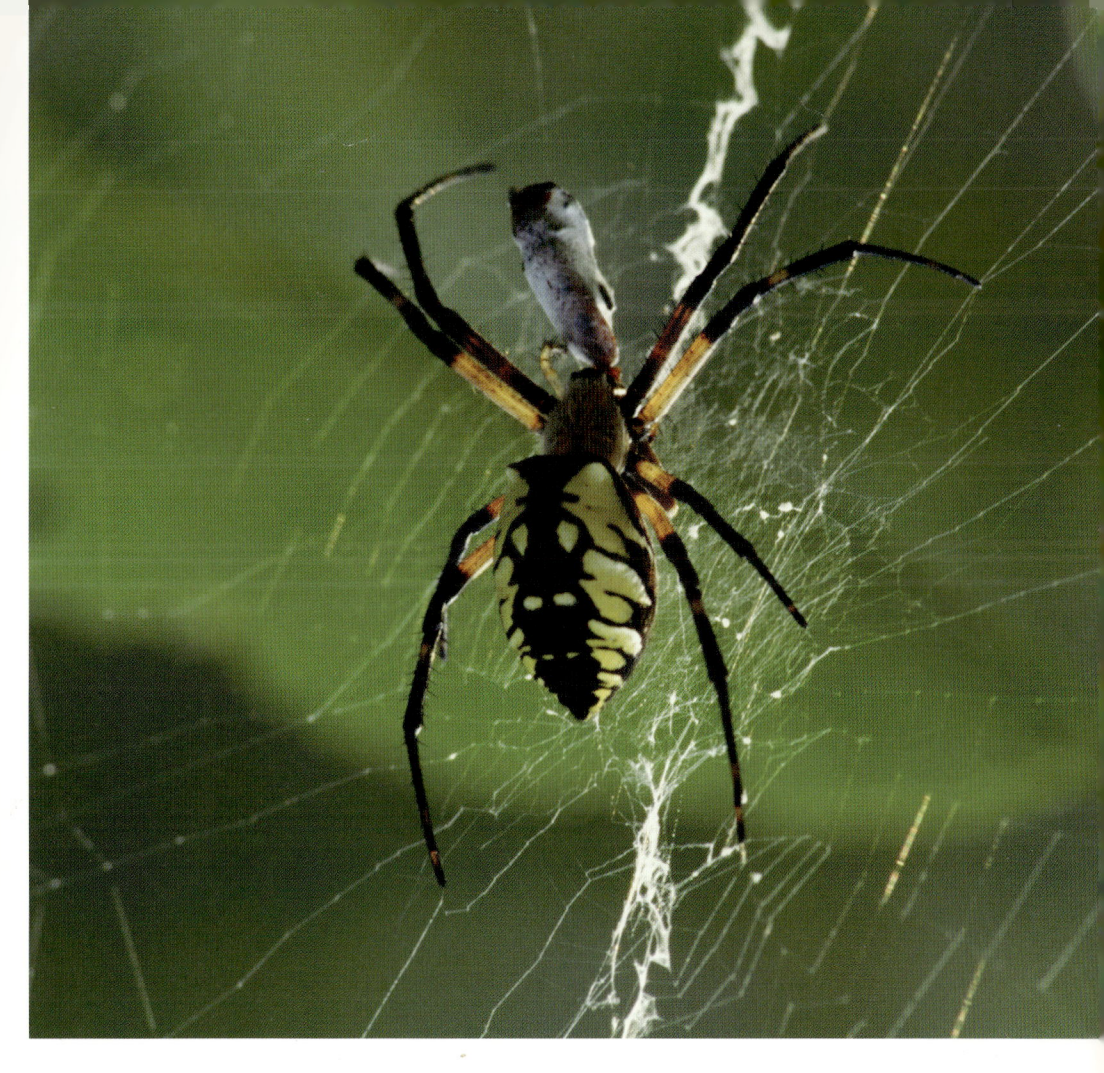

Spiders

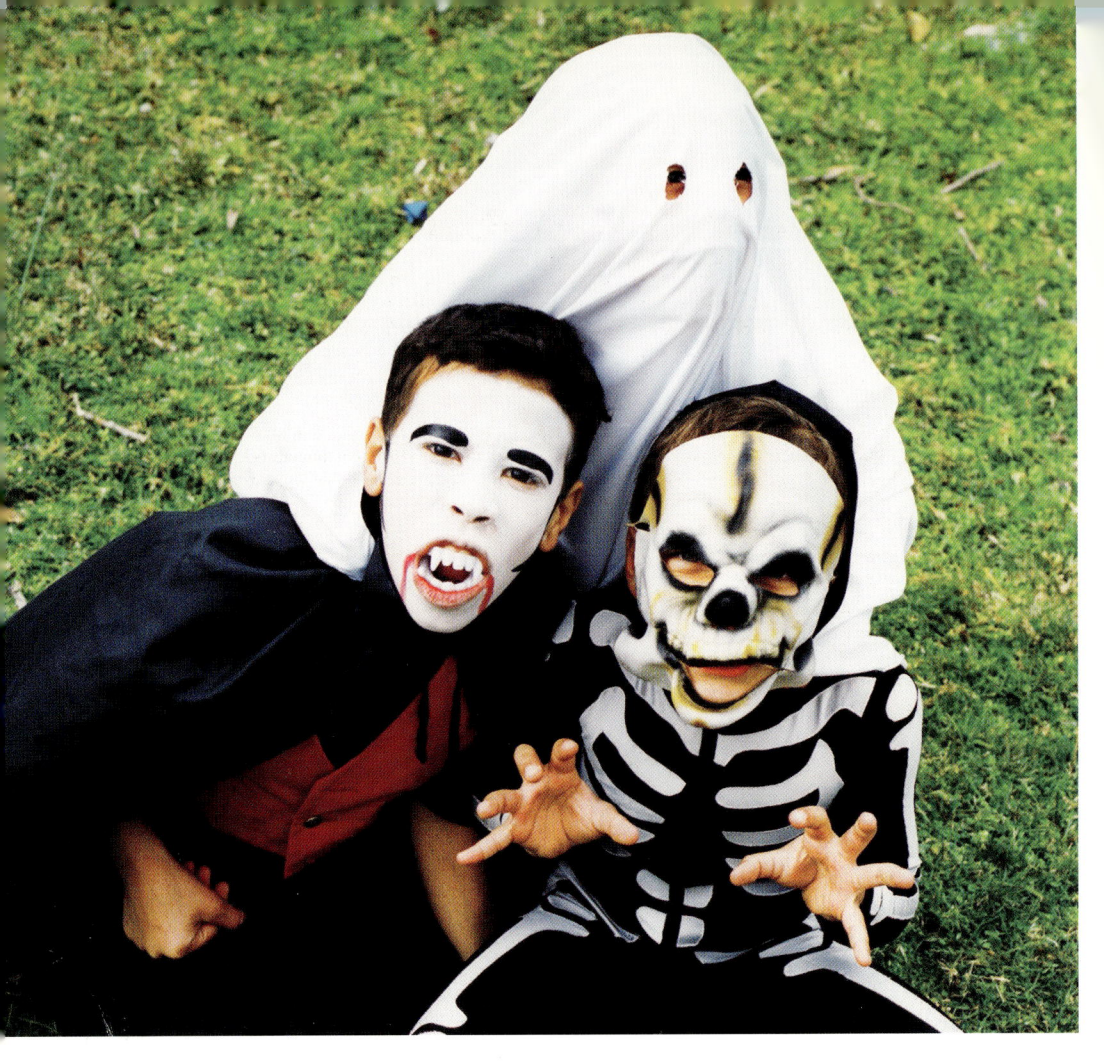

What makes you afraid?

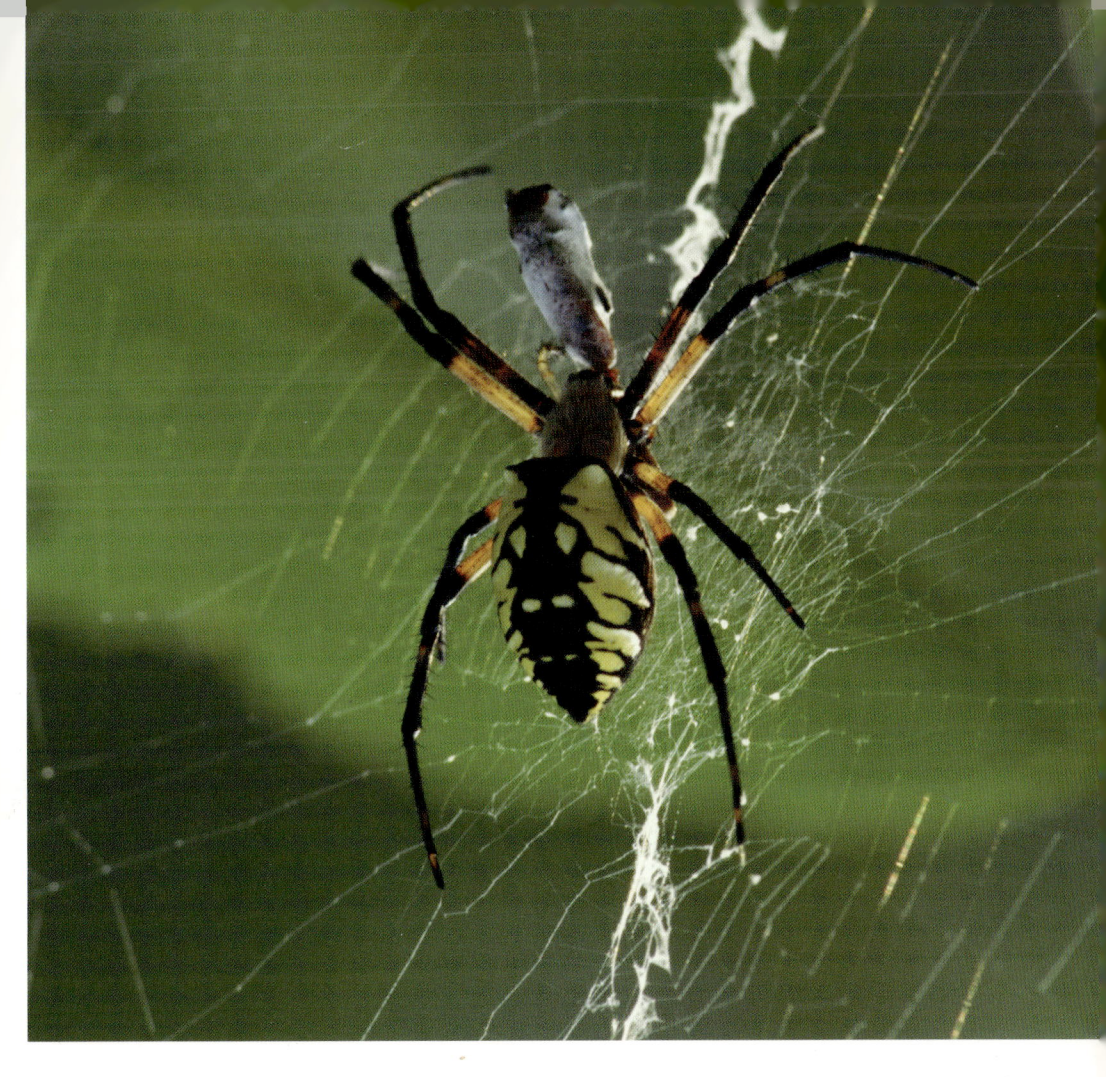

Spiders

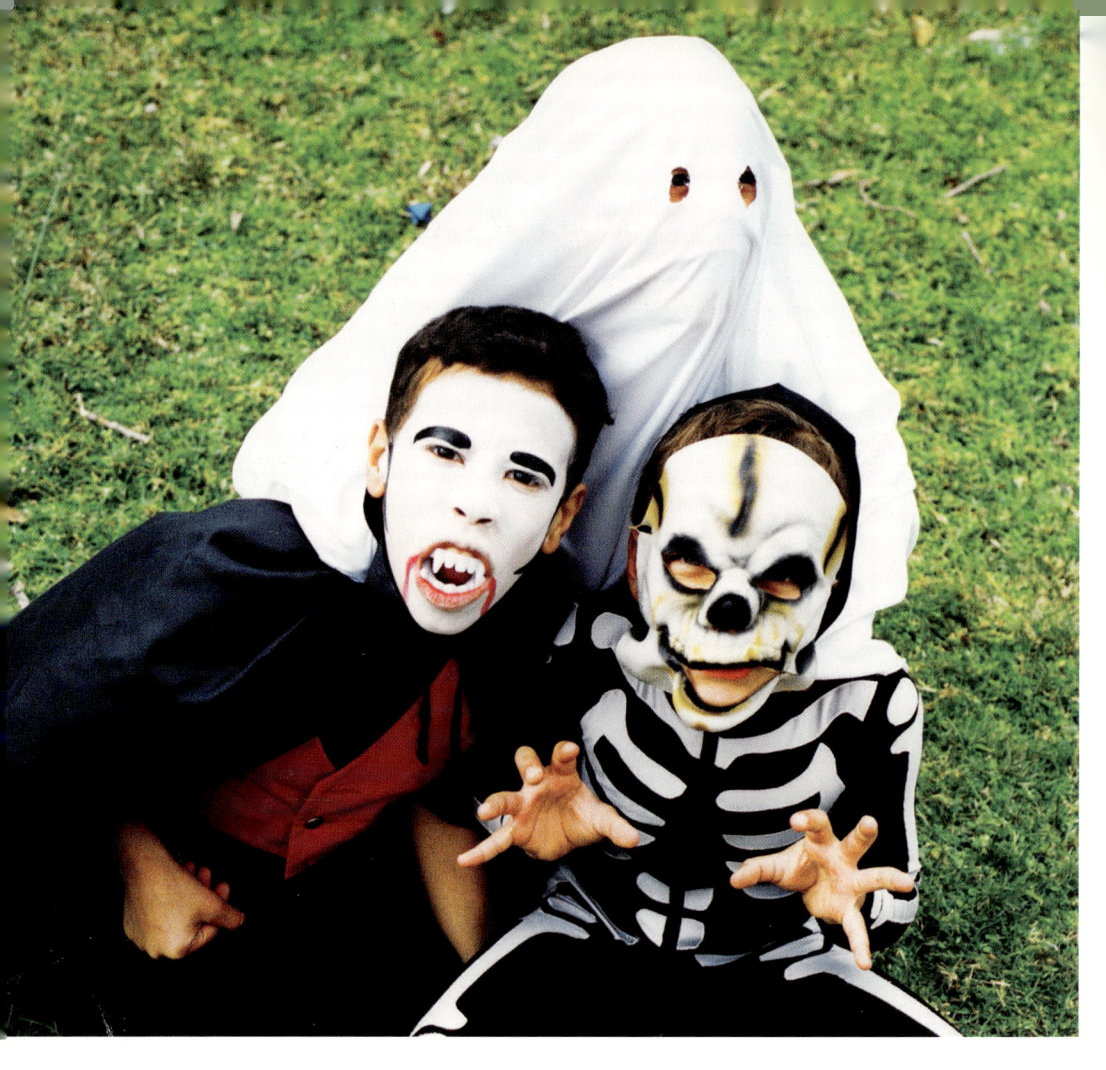

What makes you afraid?